ENIGMAS *of* HISTORY

THE MYSTERIES OF THE AMAZON RAIN FOREST

WORLD BOOK

a Scott Fetzer company
Chicago
www.worldbook.com

World Book edition of "Enigmas de la historia" by Editorial Sol 90.

Enigmas de la historia
Las ciudades perdidas del Amazonas

This edition licensed from Editorial Sol 90 S.L.
Copyright 2013 Editorial Sol S.L. All rights reserved.

Revised printing, 2016
English-language revised edition copyright 2015
World Book, Inc.
Enigmas of History
The Mysteries of the Amazon Rain Forest

World Book, Inc.
180 North LaSalle Street
Suite 900
Chicago, Illinois 60601
USA

For information about other World Book publications, visit
our website at **www.worldbook.com** or call **1-800-967-5325.**

Library of Congress Cataloging-in-Publication Data

Ciudades perdidas del Amazonas. English.
 The mysteries of the Amazon rain forest. -- English-
language revised edition.
    pages cm -- (Enigmas of history)
  Summary: "An exploration of mysteries concerning the
Amazon rain forest that have puzzled scholars, explorers,
and experts. Discusses evidence for large, pre-Columbian
urban areas in the Amazon and why such urban centers
went undiscovered for so long. Features include maps, fact
boxes, biographies of famous experts on Amazonian
culture, places to see and visit, a glossary, further
readings, and index"-- Provided by publisher.
  Includes index.
  ISBN 978-0-7166-2671-8
  1. Extinct cities--Amazon River Valley--Juvenile literature.
2. Amazon River Valley--History, Local--Juvenile literature. 3. Amazon River Valley--History--Juvenile literature.
4. Amazon River Valley--Antiquities--Juvenile literature.
5. Amazon River Valley--Civilization--Juvenile literature.
I. World Book, Inc. II. Title.
F2546.C4813 2015
985'.44--dc23
                          2015009082
Enigmas of History Set ISBN: 978-0-7166-2670-1

Revised printing, 2016
Printed in China by Shenzhen Donnelley
Printing Co., Ltd., Guangdong Province
2nd printing June 2016

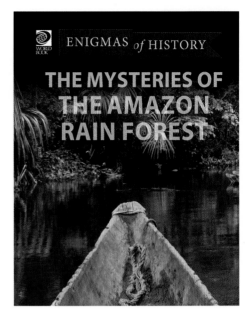

A dugout canoe glides through the Amazon
rain forest.

© Pete Oxford, Minden Pictures

Staff

Glossary There is a glossary of terms on page 44. Terms defined in the glossary are in boldface **(type that looks like this)** on their first appearance on any *spread* (two facing pages). Words that are difficult to say are followed by a pronunciation (pruh NUHN see AY shuhn) the first time they are mentioned.

Contents

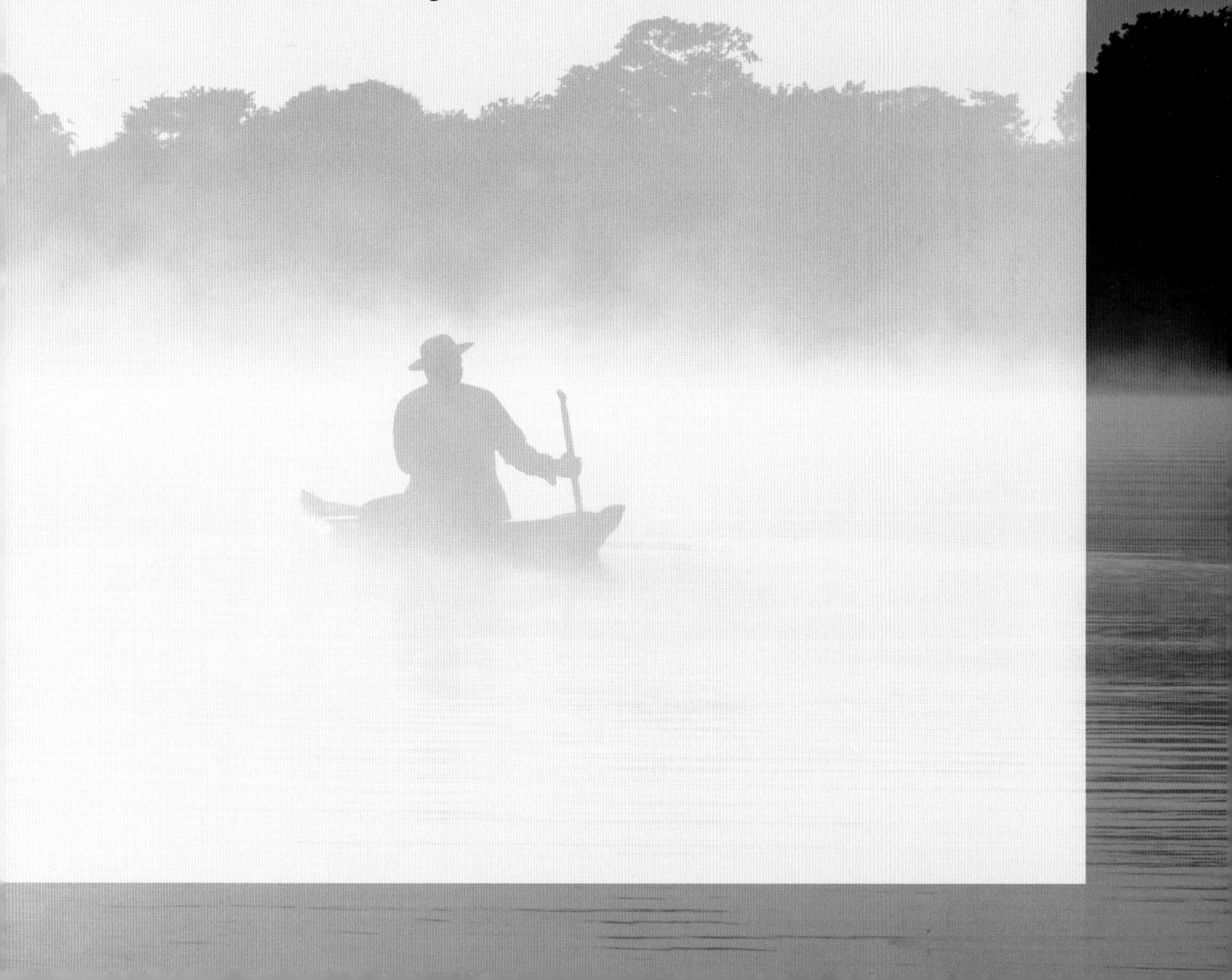

The Amazon Rain Forest: An Empty Paradise?

The Amazon **Basin** (land drained by a river) represents one of the last areas of untouched nature on the planet. This region has remained virtually uninhabited and unchanged for thousands of years because of dense jungle conditions holding back human settlement. At least, this image was the observation of the Europeans who traveled through this region in the 1700's. They told stories of crossing vast sections of rain forest with few signs of human life. **Anthropologists** (scientists who study human culture) and naturalists subsequently confirmed this idea up until the beginning of the 1900's.

However, the few documents available that discuss the Amazon, written by Spanish and Portuguese explorers during the 1500's and 1600's, speak of large settlements made up of thousands of people, located along the length of the Amazon River and its major **tributaries.** And at the end of the 1800's, the first scientific expeditions to the Amazon River **estuary** and the Central Amazon seemed to back up the accounts of these **conquistadors** (Spanish conquerors).

How is this explained? The **indigenous** peoples of the New World, including those in the Amazon, had very low levels of **immunity** (resistance) against most of the diseases brought by the Europeans, such as influenza, measles, and smallpox. The rapid spread of these diseases throughout the Amazon Basin caused the disappearance of entire groups long before any Europeans met them. In addition, rocky outcrops of stone that can be used for building are uncommon in the Amazon. Homes were constructed of wood and *thatch* (woven straw or palm leaves). Earth was the main raw material used by the ancient peoples of the Amazon Basin to build such structures as irrigation canals or religious sites. To the untrained eye, it would have been difficult to tell the difference between natural formations and structures built by humans, such as earthen **embankments.** The difficulty increases when these structures are covered by the dense plants of the rain forest.

Archaeologists (scientists who study past cultures) today know that the modern image of the Amazon as an unoccupied and uninhabitable region is likely not correct. This image resulted from a number of historical factors. Local populations died off rapidly as disease spread in the 1500's. Rain forest growth then rapidly covered areas that had been previously occupied, hiding structures and other signs of human occupation. In addition, the end of the 1800's and beginning of the 1900's was a difficult time for the remaining indigenous peoples of the Amazon. They were often used as slaves at rubber tree plantations. As a result, a **nomadic** (wandering) lifestyle with small, widely spread out villages became natural for the people. This way of life was an adaptation to then-present historical conditions rather than a long tradition among people of the Amazon.

In recent decades, in nearly every area of the Amazon jungle investigated by archaeologists, evidence of humans having lived there has been found. Today archaeologists believe that the Amazon has been occupied for as long as 14,000 years by various peoples. These ranged from nomadic hunter-gatherers to permanent groups that created sophisticated tools and objects from stone and *ceramic* (pottery).

Perhaps the greatest treasure given to us by these peoples, ancestors of the tribes of the Amazon today, is their sophisticated knowledge of the rich and complex environment of the Amazon.

Archaeologists have worked to understand how this natural world has been transformed. To these researchers, the Amazon Basin, its history, and its development over the centuries must be considered in light of a combination of factors. Natural factors (animals, plants, and minerals) and human contributions have greatly affected the Amazon over time. This consideration is all the more urgent today because the Amazon's natural resources and native peoples are threatened from environmental destruction caused by such actions as **deforestation** (clearing trees) and mining.

The Lost Cities of the Amazon

The Amazon, one of the least explored areas on the planet, is beginning to reveal its secrets. Recent research appears to confirm the existence of complex **civilizations** made up of thousands of people.

Until recently, most scholars believed that jungles surrounding the Amazon—the largest and widest river in the world—only provided enough resources for small, widely scattered groups of hunter-gatherers. Yet, indications that these lands were once home to thousands of people, including complex, structured **societies** (groups) for hundreds, maybe thousands, of years, have begun to come to light.

NEW EVIDENCE

Such scientists as Clark L. Erickson of the University of Pennsylvania; Brazilian Eduardo Neves, of the University of São Paulo; and Colombian Augusto Oyuela-Caycedo and German Michael Heckenberger, both from the University of Florida, have explored and made important discoveries. Some of their sites include San Martín de Samiria, the region around the Madeira River in northwest Bolivia; Manaus, in central Brazil; the territory around the Xingu River, in southern Brazil; and Marajó Island at the mouth of the Amazon.

In all of these areas, scientists have found evidence indicating the presence of an advanced **culture** (way of life) that would have been capable of supporting thousands of people in an area where, until recently, scholars would have considered the land to be incapable of supplying the resources necessary to build a complex society.

In San Martín de Samiria, Augusto Oyuela-Caycedo found evidence of human occupation dating back to A.D. 900. The remains of orchards and **agricultural** (farming) fields with mounds of enriched earth were discovered here. These lands could have provided food crops for as many as 5,000 people.

At sites in northern Bolivia near the Madeira River and stretching as far as Acre in Brazil, American, Finnish, and South American scientists have found mounds of **fertile** soil, **raised fields**, large roads, and water canals that date to around A.D. 1200. In this area, **deforestation** has made it possible to see many enigmatic **geoglyphs,** often circular or rectangular. The geoglyphs cannot easily be constructed or even seen in forest areas, and researchers believe that people must have made them at a time when the region had few trees.

In the Amazon near Manaus, Brazil, Eduardo Neves also found evidence of orchards and soils fertilized with plant remains, human waste, and other materials. The remains of a large open plaza and other earthen works that date from between A.D. 970 and 1440 were also found. Near this location, at Painted Rock Cave, only 6 miles (9.6 kilometers) from the Amazon River, **archaeologists** in 1992 discovered stone tools and other remains demonstrating that humans first arrived and occupied this region between 10,000 and 11,200 years ago.

Along the Xingu River, one of the Amazon's Brazilian **tributaries,** Heckenberger has studied what seems to be networks of trenches, **embankments,** roads, and canals. Heckenberger believes these to be the remains of a **civilization** that existed as early as A.D. 800, well before the arrival of Spanish explorers in the **New World.**

At Marajó Island, in the Amazon **estuary,** researchers have found remains of pottery, building foundations, and signs of **agricultural** fields that may have been capable of feeding 100,000 people.

All this evidence adds weight to the theory that the Amazon has long been inhabited by complex, technologically developed societies with large populations. These **societies** were able to tame the rain forest around them and provide food for the thousands of people living in wooden buildings in busy **urban** (city) centers connected by a network of roads.

RESISTANCE
Not all researchers agree with the idea that large, complex societies inhabited the Amazon **Basin.** Betty J. Meggers (1921-2012), former director of Latin American Archaeology at the Smithsonian Institute in Washington, D.C., asserted in her book *Man and Culture in a Counterfeit Paradise* (1971) that the Amazon is not and has never been suitable for sustaining large groups of people. Meggers believed that such theories are not supported by evidence, for example, as pollen preserved in the soil, that would indicate large-scale agriculture in the prehistoric Amazon. She suggested that some regions may have supported modest human populations, but most of the Amazon was uninhabited.

However, to other scientists, such as Eduardo Neves, recent discoveries are providing exciting new evidence about a neglected region and period of South American history.

IN SEARCH OF "EL DORADO"
The search for ancient cities in the Amazon is not new. In fact, Spanish and British explorers have made many attempts to locate El Dorado, a mythical kingdom where the streets were paved in gold that was reported to exist in the Amazon. In 1535, Spaniard Sebastián de Belalcázar sought El Dorado in the area near what is now Colombia. Gonzalo Jiménez de Quesada searched for the fabled city in the Muisca territory of Brazil beginning in 1569.

The most famous expedition was the one led by Gonzalo Pizarro and Francisco de Orellana in 1541. The two set out from Quito, Ecuador, and headed east. Pizarro and his men soon returned to Quito, while Orellana continued in with a group of 50 men to where the Trinidad and Napo rivers met. Pushed by the currents, they entered an even larger river. During the journey, the crew was attacked by what appeared to be female Indian warriors. The Spaniards called their attackers Amazons, after female warriors of Greek mythology. This name later was given to the newly discovered river and the nearby area. They reached the Amazon River's outlet to the Atlantic Ocean in 1542.

Gaspar de Carvajal, a Dominican missionary who traveled with Orellana, authored an account of this

Francisco de Orellana

Gonzalo Jiménez de Quesada

Sebastián de Belalcázar

Gonzalo Pizarro

MANOA odel DORA

EL DORADO

Illustration from 1599 showing the mythical city of El Dorado, located on the banks of the imaginary lake Parime, near the Essequibo River in Guyana.

EXPEDITIONS

In the 1500's, several Spanish **conquistadors** launched expeditions to the eastern slopes of the Andes in search of El Dorado.

expedition titled *Relación del nuevo descubrimiento del famoso río Grande que descubrió por muy gran ventura el capitán Francisco de Orellana* (Account of the Recent Discovery of the Famous Grand River, which Was Discovered by Great Good Fortune by Captain Francisco de Orellana). The account provides interesting information about the **rituals,** customs, tools, and military tactics of the natives they met along the way. The missionary writes of "shining cities," "canoes holding dozens of warriors," "straight, well-traveled avenues," and "very **fertile** lands." Gaspar de Carvajal's testimony was dismissed over the years by those who considered it as fantasies and exaggerations written to attract colonists to Peru.

However, the recent discoveries in the Amazon back up the missionary's account from the 1500's. Researchers now understand that there were large, straight "avenues" and communities populated by hundreds, perhaps thousands, of people among fertile agricultural fields.

But were there cities? If so, they could not have been built of stone. From the river, it could be that Carvajal saw large wooden buildings behind protective **palisades** (fences).

PAITITI: A LEGEND?

European explorers sought another fantastic city called Paititi, said to be found in the mountain plains in the border region of southeastern Peru, northern Bolivia, and southwestern

Brazil. Popular legend claims that Paititi was built by the Incas, who retreated into the jungle with all the treasures of the empire after Spanish **conquistadors** arrived.

Various tales claim that during the time of the Incas, the jungle surrounding the Madre de Dios River was called Antisuyo, and its inhabitants were called Antis. The Andes Mountains are named for these people. It is said that the Incas conquered the tribes and forced them to pay a tribute in gold. An Inca legend tells that the hero Inkarri founded a great city called Paititi in the jungle here long before the arrival of the Spaniards.

After the Spanish arrived in 1533, the Inca Prince Huascar is said to have transferred all the riches of the Inca to Paititi for safe keeping. The city was to be the last stronghold of the Inca civilization following Spanish conquest of the empire.

Another version of the legend places Paititi much further east, on what is now the border between Bolivia and Brazil. This area was inhabited by the Mojo tribe for centuries. In their language, called Arawak, *paititi* means "white and shining." In this same area of the Bolivian Amazon, called the Moxos Plains, **archaeologists** have found **geoglyphs,** remains of canals, and walls attributed to ancient Amazon peoples.

EUROPEAN SOURCES

Some written accounts of the search for these legendary cities exist. One account is by the Roman Catholic priest Andrea López, from around 1600. He wrote of a large city, which he claimed was rich in gold, silver, and jewels, located in the middle of the jungle "near a waterfall called Paititi by the natives." This written account was first discovered by the Italian archaeologist Mario Polia in

2001, in an archive in Rome.

Another account from 1618 is also attributed to a Catholic priest, Blas Valera. He is believed to be the author of *Exsul Immeritus Blas Valera Populo Suo* (The Wrongful Exile of Blas Valera). This account of his travels includes two **engravings** depicting the city of Paititi from the jungle and from the mountain. This document was found in 1999 by Italian scholar Laura Laurencich Minelli among the papers of a private collector in Naples, Italy.

Researchers have not ruled out the existence of Inca cities that may still be hidden in the jungle. They know that the Inca empire maintained an active presence in the western Amazon. Ties between tribes and communities from the South American coast to the mountains and the jungle were strong and complex.

Archaeologists have discovered paved roads built by the Inca that enter the Amazon jungle, and they suspect that others remain undiscovered. However, some explorers, including the Spaniard Juan Álvarez Maldonado, who trekked through the Peruvian jungle in 1568, thought the name Paititi was simply a native name for the Amazon River.

Legends of lost cities of the Amazon continued to inspire adventurers well into modern times. Percy Fawcett (see pages 20-23), an officer in the British Army, was one such adventurer. In 1906, the Royal Geographical Society invited Fawcett to *survey* (map) the frontier between Brazil and Bolivia. He spent months there and learned much about the peoples of the jungle. After World War I, Fawcett returned to Brazil, fascinated by stories of an unnamed hidden city described in a document called Manuscript 512 from the 1700's. Fawcett went looking for this city, which he called "Z," in 1925, and he was never heard from again.

Clark L. Erickson
(1955 -   )

To Clark Erickson, of the University of Pennsylvania, the vast Amazon jungle in Peru and Bolivia represents a landscape crisscrossed with signs of human activity in the form of raised fields, causeways, and other massive earthworks. Erickson's experimental farm projects in South America have investigated whether techniques used by ancient peoples of the Amazon can be used to grow food today.

AERIAL VIEWS In his work, Erickson analyzes satellite images and photos from airplanes to identify such landscape features as canals and causeways in the Amazon basin.

Augusto Oyuela-Caycedo
(1969 -   )

Having earned a doctorate in archaeology in the United States, this Colombian professor teaches at the University of Florida and is an expert in the ecological history of the Upper Amazon—shared by Colombia, Peru, and Brazil.

ECOLOGY His findings have caused scholars to question their belief in an unaltered and continuous culture in the Amazon Jungle.

Denise Schaan
(1956 -)

A specialist on the **ceramics** of Marajó Island, this Brazilian archaeologist has made important discoveries concerning the Marajó culture. She has also studied the geoglyphs at Alto Purús in the Amazon forest of Peru. Schaan thinks the geoglyphs represent the remains of ritual centers.

CIVILIZATION In her work, Schaan states that the sophisticated Marajó culture was not an isolated phenomenon in the Amazon Basin.

Michael Heckenberger
(1963 -)

A specialist in the historical evolution of tribal **societies** in the Amazon, this **anthropologist** and archaeologist from the University of Florida studied the Kuikuro, residents of the Upper Xingu, a tributary of the Amazon River in Brazil. He believes they are the heirs of an ancient farming culture that developed deep in the jungle. Michael Heckenberger maintains that complex societies existed in the Amazon region before the arrival of the Europeans. As an anthropologist, he has described the social systems at the heart of the Kuikuro culture and their village structure, which includes the construction of trenches, avenues, and bridges. The author of such works as *The Enigma of the Great Cities*,

Heckenberger maintains that, in accordance with archaeological findings, between about A.D. 800 and 1300, the inhabitants of the Upper Xingu made up a complex society ten times larger than that of today, characterized by villages built in clusters, in geometric patterns, with a larger village and a plaza in the middle. Roads connected them all. Heckenberger compares them in sophistication to villages in Europe during the Middle Ages.

INNOVATOR Heckenberger is one of the leading exponents of the new current of investigation that defends the existence of a level of urbanization in pre-Columbian Amazonia comparable to that of medieval Europe.

> *"They may not have had the technical or social command of the Romans or Incas, but the Amazon peoples were as capable of innovating as any other people in the world.*
>
> Michael Heckenberger

Eduardo Neves (1966 -)

Brazilian archaeologist and historian Eduardo Neves is known for his research on human occupation of the Amazon in ancient times. A professor at the Museum of Archaeology and Ethnology belonging to the University of São Paulo and the Federal University of the Amazon, he has written several books and many articles about his archaeological work, mainly carried

out in the Manaus region of central Brazil. Neves and Heckenberger are the leading proponents of the theory that the Amazon Basin teemed with large, complex societies that were all but obliterated by disease when European colonists arrived after 1492.

TERRA PRETA Neves is of the opinion that the fertility of the *terra preta* is the result of human action, and that it could have sustained a complex pre-Columbian Amazonian society.

Remnants of Civilization

Since the 1960's, **archaeologists** have investigated the Amazon. Before them, **conquistadors** and adventurers trekked through the region searching for magnificent cities of gold. In the course of these expeditions, people have discovered evidence in the form of occupation sites, oil deposits, and agricultural fields, which scholars believe provide proof of a complex **civilization** that once existed in the Amazon River Basin.

Findings in the jungle

Over the past 500 years, conquerors, explorers, and adventurers have gone to the Amazon Basin in search of lost cities built by a civilization that disappeared without leaving any trace. For many archaeologists, evidence discovered in recent decades strongly supports the idea that there was a complex, developed civilization in the Amazon region. While they may not have built cities of gold, these cultures learned to live with, and even thrive, in the rain forest.

Magnified area

PACIFIC OCEAN

VENEZUELA

COLOMBIA

Negro River

Quito

ECUADOR

Napo River

Japurá River

Amazon River

San Martín de Tipishca

1

Juruá River

River Purus

Talara

Trujillo

Porto Velho

5

PERU

Lima

BOLIVIA

2
El Beni Region

La Paz

1 San Martín de Tipishca

One of the larger towns of the nearly 100 settlements in the Pacaya Samiria National Reserve, where archaeologists have found evidence of villages, cultivation of fruit trees, and enriched soils that date to around A.D. 900. The villages could have housed some 5,000 people.

2 El Beni, Bolivia

Archaeologists working in this region of northern Bolivia have discovered **raised fields** for **agriculture** connected by **causeways** and channels that date to around A.D. 1200. They estimate that the fields could have supported a population as large as 25,000 people.

3 Xingu National Park

Located in the state of Mato Grosso, Brazil, this park was created to protect **indigenous** tribes that still reside in the rain forest. But the park also houses remains of a series of ancient urban centers connected by pathways, which suggest to archaeologists that an ancient civilization existed in the region.

How Widespread Was the Amazon Civilization?

In the Amazon Basin, archaeologists have found evidence of sophisticated techniques to increase soil **fertility,** similar to those seen in the Moxos Plains of Bolivia. These techniques permit nutrient-poor rain forest soils to be turned into productive agricultural lands. Many archaeologists believe such techniques were **indigenous** developments that spread. Native peoples in both regions speak a language in the Arawak group, indicating a past connection.

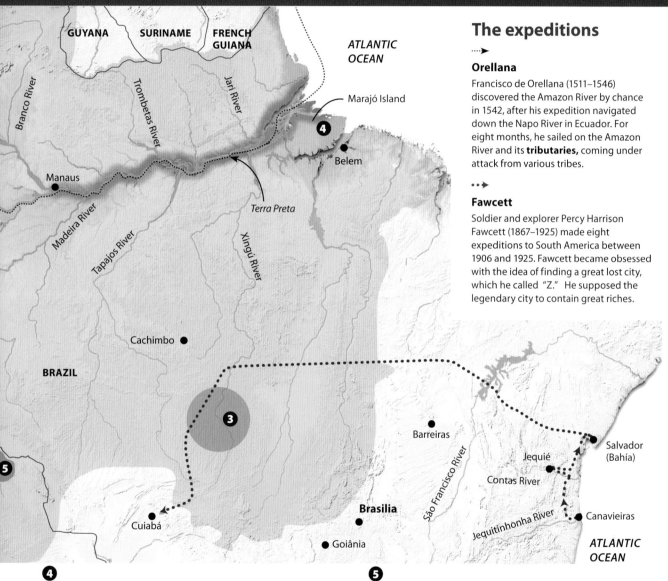

GUYANA   SURINAME   FRENCH GUIANA

ATLANTIC OCEAN

Branco River
Trombetas River
Jari River

Marajó Island

Belem

Manaus

Madeira River

Terra Preta

Tapajos River

Xingú River

Cachimbo

BRAZIL

❸

Barreiras

São Francisco River

Jequié

Salvador (Bahía)

Contas River

Brasilia

Cuiabá

Goiânia

Jequitinhonha River

Canavieiras

ATLANTIC OCEAN

❺

The expeditions

····➤

Orellana

Francisco de Orellana (1511–1546) discovered the Amazon River by chance in 1542, after his expedition navigated down the Napo River in Ecuador. For eight months, he sailed on the Amazon River and its **tributaries,** coming under attack from various tribes.

··➤

Fawcett

Soldier and explorer Percy Harrison Fawcett (1867–1925) made eight expeditions to South America between 1906 and 1925. Fawcett became obsessed with the idea of finding a great lost city, which he called "Z." He supposed the legendary city to contain great riches.

❹

Marajó Island

Here on the world's largest river island, archaeologists discovered thousands of pottery *shards* (pieces). The pottery's style is distinct compared with other **ceramic** styles found in the Amazon. The amount of pottery found suggests that an urban center that may have housed up to 100,000 people once thrived here.

❺

Geoglyphs

Deforestation in Bolivia and Brazil revealed huge **geoglyphs** hidden by rain forest growth for hundreds of years. Many of the geoglyphs are connected by roads. Some archaeologists believe they were constructed by a sophisticated **culture** that inhabited the region before European contact.

Did the City of El Dorado Exist?

El Dorado, the mythical city of gold, has never been found. Nonetheless, numerous accounts from the 1500's were written about its existence. Could the remains found in the Amazon be linked to this city? The mystery continues....

The legend of El Dorado originated in Peru during the time of the first Spanish **conquistadors.** Natives told tales to the conquerors, who were obsessed with gold, of a place where the precious metal was so common that the inhabitants ignored it. This fantastic place, possibly located somewhere in what is now central Colombia, was said to be a location for sacred ceremonies in which the natives offered gold and emeralds to their gods.

The Spanish writer Juan Rodríguez Freyle (1566-1640) wrote of such tales in *Conquista y Descubrimiento del Nuevo Reino de Granada de las Indias Occidentales del Mar Océano* (Conquest and Discovery of the New Kingdom of Granada of the West Indies Sea), in 1636. This work is a **chronicle** (written history) of the events relating to the colonization of Colombia. In this book, Rodríguez Freyle tells of ceremonies among the Muisca people involving priests who were literally covered in gold dust. In another account, directed to the Spanish Governor of Guatavita, he states that "in Lake Guatavita, they make a raft of reeds [...] remove the chief's clothing [...] smear him with sticky sand, and sprinkle everything with gold dust, so that he is completely covered with this metal. They put him on the raft, which is tied, and place a great pile of gold and emeralds at his feet to be offered to their god [...] The golden native presents their offering by throwing all the gold and emeralds at his feet into the lake...."

Many explorers have searched Colombia, Brazil, Ecuador, Peru, and Venezuela for the wonderful city of El Dorado without success. Many scholars consider El Dorado a myth. However, in 1969, some farmers made a discovery in a cave in the Colombian municipality of Pasca that lends some support to the fantastic tale reported by Freyle. Inside a **ceramic** vessel, they found a small figurine made of pure gold by Muisca artisans. This figurine, known as the Muisca Raft (see page 19), has a central figure wearing a large

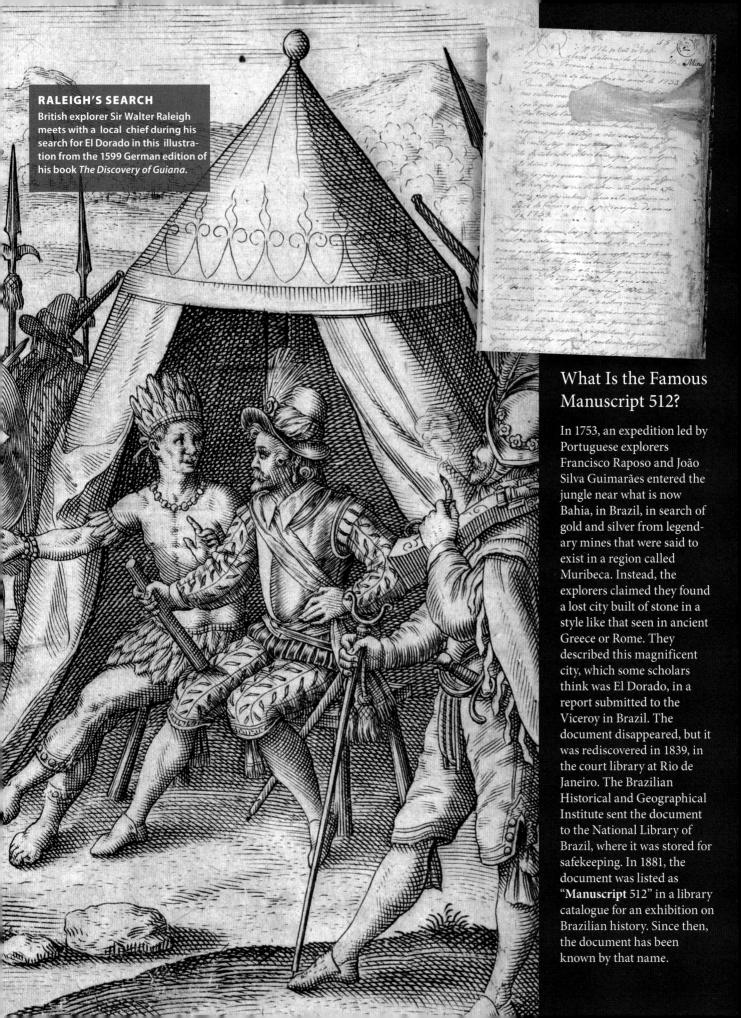

What Is the Famous Manuscript 512?

In 1753, an expedition led by Portuguese explorers Francisco Raposo and João Silva Guimarães entered the jungle near what is now Bahia, in Brazil, in search of gold and silver from legendary mines that were said to exist in a region called Muribeca. Instead, the explorers claimed they found a lost city built of stone in a style like that seen in ancient Greece or Rome. They described this magnificent city, which some scholars think was El Dorado, in a report submitted to the Viceroy in Brazil. The document disappeared, but it was rediscovered in 1839, in the court library at Rio de Janeiro. The Brazilian Historical and Geographical Institute sent the document to the National Library of Brazil, where it was stored for safekeeping. In 1881, the document was listed as **"Manuscript 512"** in a library catalogue for an exhibition on Brazilian history. Since then, the document has been known by that name.

European Greed

European adventurers from other nations searched for the legendary El Dorado as well. Germans Nikolaus Federmann, Georg von Speyer, and Philipp von Hutten were among the first explorers attracted by the legend. They were employed by the Welsers, a German banking family who provided funds for King Charles I of Spain. Between 1535 and 1538, they led expeditions to the territories of New Granada, in what is now Venezuela and Colombia, searching for the fabulous city of gold.

The legend of El Dorado also enticed enemies of the Spanish to explore the region. In 1595, English soldier and explorer Sir Walter Raleigh explored what is now Guyana and eastern Venezuela with his crew in the service of Queen Elizabeth I. He had heard that El Dorado could be found in an unexplored jungle region at the head of the Caroni River, a tributary of the Orinoco River. However, he failed to find the

fabulous city. Hoping to repair his damaged reputation upon his return to England, Raleigh wrote *The Discovery of Guiana* in 1595, an account of the journey in which he made exaggerated claims about his discoveries. Raleigh's book did more to spread the legend of El Dorado throughout Europe than any other source.

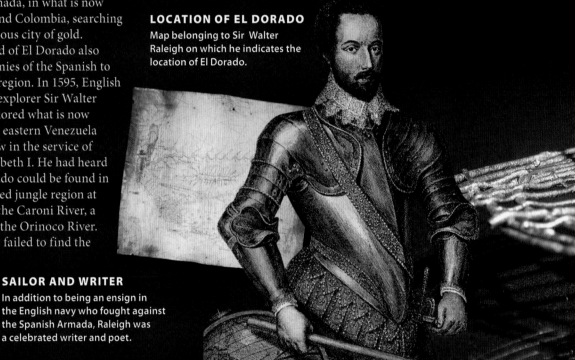

LOCATION OF EL DORADO
Map belonging to Sir Walter Raleigh on which he indicates the location of El Dorado.

SAILOR AND WRITER
In addition to being an ensign in the English navy who fought against the Spanish Armada, Raleigh was a celebrated writer and poet.

headdress with various other figures surrounding him on a raft. The Muisca Raft, which measures about 8 inches by 4 inches (20 centimeters by 10 centimeters), depicts the same ceremony held at Lake Guatavita that was described by Freyle. The raft was made sometime between about A.D. 1200 and 1500. Today, this rare piece of art is displayed in the Gold Museum in Bogotá, Colombia.

SIMILAR RITUALS
The **ritual** illustrated by the Muisca Raft was likely celebrated among other native groups in the northern

Amazon. In 1856, a gold piece similar to the Muisca Raft was found in the Siecha Lagoons in Colombia. The gold piece supports this theory.

Descriptions of the object are rare. But, an **engraving** of the Siecha Raft was published in 1882 in the book *El Dorado* by Liborio Zerda. The engraving was enough to reawaken scientific interest in El Dorado worldwide. The Siecha Raft was later acquired by a German museum. Unfortunately, the gold raft, which weighed only about 6 ounces (170 grams), was lost when the transport ship was destroyed in a fire upon its

arrival in Bremen, Germany, so it cannot be studied today.

Scholars now believe that several tribes in what is now Colombia likely held rituals in which the chief, covered in gold dust and gems, made offerings to the gods by jumping into a lake. To these scholars, it seems that this region, inhabited since pre-Hispanic times by the Muisca people, gave rise to the legend of El Dorado. Spanish treasure hunters attempted to drain Lake Guatavita to reach the treasures they believed were hidden in its depths. Today, there remains a large trench on one side of the lake

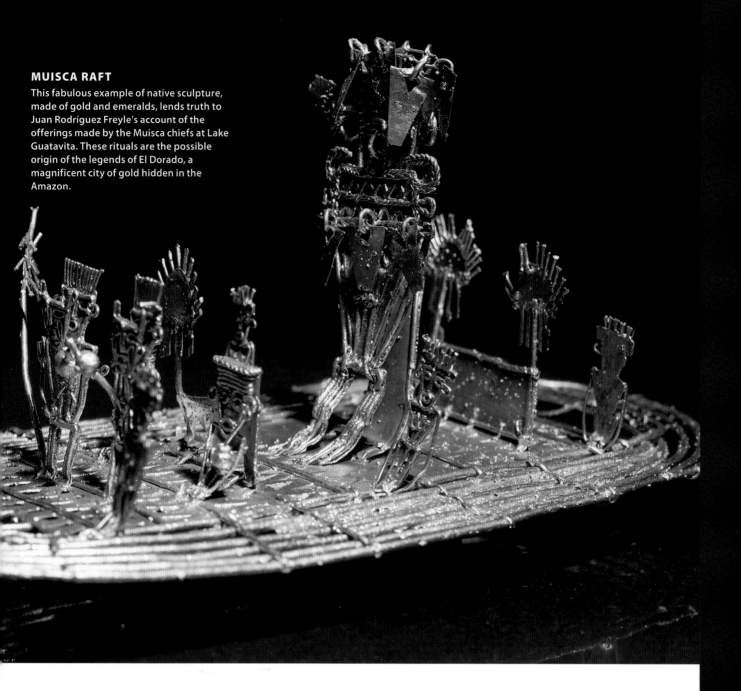

MUISCA RAFT
This fabulous example of native sculpture, made of gold and emeralds, lends truth to Juan Rodríguez Freyle's account of the offerings made by the Muisca chiefs at Lake Guatavita. These rituals are the possible origin of the legends of El Dorado, a magnificent city of gold hidden in the Amazon.

that some historians date to 1580 which was made by treasure hunters.

Divers who explored the lake and investigated the trench in 1990 found that the lake had been drained between 1900 and 1906. No gold objects were found at the time. The Siecha **Lagoons** were also drained several times in the colonial period, but no treasure was found.

EXPEDITIONS
On more than a dozen expeditions in the 1500's, Spanish explorers search-ed for El Dorado, beginning with Diego de Ordaz's expedition in

1530 and finishing with Domingo Vera's expedition in 1596. In between were Gonzalo Pizarro's quest in 1539 and the three expeditions led by Pedro de Silva, in 1566, 1568, and 1570.

The English also sought the legendary city. The first attempt was by Sir Walter Raleigh, who sailed up the Orinoco to the interior of Guyana in 1595. However, he had no luck finding the legendary kingdom.

Later, the English equated El Dorado with the legend of Paititi, the hidden Inca stronghold, described in **Manuscript** 512. In 1913, British

explorer O'Sullivan Beare claimed to have seen a city of gold from a distance on the right bank of the San Francisco River, some 12 days by horse from Salvador, in Bahia, Brazil. Beare told his story to British Colonel Percy Fawcett, who, in 1921, organized an expedition to the Sincora Mountains and Orobó River in western Brazil. Fawcett found inscriptions on rocks similar to those described in Manuscript 512, but no trace of "the lost city of Z." He also failed to find the lost city on his last expedition to the Upper Xingu in 1925, from which he did not return.

Fawcett's Final Expedition

In 1925, Colonel Percy Fawcett ventured into the Amazon jungle in what he called "the greatest exploration mystery of the twentieth century."

Explorers and adventurers have been lured into the Amazon jungle by legends of magnificent lost cities of gold since the first Europeans set eyes on the place nearly 500 years ago. Perhaps none are so famous as Colonel Percy H. Fawcett, who ventured into the Amazon jungle in 1925 in search of a legendary city of gold he believed could be found somewhere in the vast Mato Grosso region of Brazil. Percy Harrison Fawcett was born in Devon, United Kingdom, in 1867. He served in the British Army and was a trained **surveyor** (map maker). In 1906, the Royal Geographical Society, a British organization that sponsors scientific expeditions, invited Fawcett to survey part of the frontier between Brazil and Bolivia. He spent 18 months at Mato Grosso, where he learned much about the peoples of the jungle. After serving in the military during World War I (1914-1918), Fawcett returned to Brazil in 1918. He was fascinated by stories of a hidden city, which he may have read about in the famous **Manuscript** 512. He planned an expedition into the interior Amazon Basin to discover this lost city, which he called "Z." In 1925, with his son Jack, and his son's friend Raleigh Rimell, Fawcett ventured into the jungle. In his last correspondence, a letter to his wife dated May 29, 1925, Fawcett wrote, "You need have no fear of any failure." The group was last seen crossing the Upper Xingu, a southeastern **tributary** of the Amazon. From there, they vanished without a trace.

Fawcett left instructions stating that if his expedition did not return, no rescue should be attempted. Fawcett was worried that a rescue party could suffer the same fate. He wrote: "I don't want rescue parties coming to look for us. It's too risky. If with all my experience we can't make it, there's not much hope for others. That's one reason why I'm not telling exactly where we're going."

Many scholars believe the explorers were killed by hostile natives. Or perhaps they died of disease or starvation in their fruitless search for Z. The Amazon Basin remains a dangerous place for outsiders today. In the years since Fawcett vanished, there have been at least 13 expeditions attempting to find him, and as many as 100 people have died while searching for traces of the expedition in the unforgiving jungle. But the fate of the expedition remains an unsolved mystery today. Percy Fawcett's younger son Brian wrote of the expedition in *Exploration Fawcett* (1953).

AMAZON MAP
A map that Fawcett
took with him on one
of his early expeditions
to the Amazon.

PERCY FAWCETT
This British explorer
conducted various
expeditions into the
Amazon.

The City of Z

In 1925, for the eighth time in his life, British Colonel Percy Fawcett entered the Amazon jungle. On this particular occasion, he was searching for the ruins of a lost city he called "Z," mentioned in Manuscript 512. At the end of May, the explorer mysteriously disappeared in the area of the Upper Xingu.

Final Images

This image (left) is one of the last photos taken of Percy Fawcett's 1925 expedition in search of the lost city "Z." The photograph shows a member of Fawcett's canoe exchanging information with native Kalapalos in another canoe. The Kalapalos were the last tribe to see the explorer and his companions alive.

EXPLORER   Percy Fawcett (center) with members of his expedition to find the sources of the Rio Verde, in 1908.

Amazon Urban Planning

Scientists thought that the **indigenous** peoples of the Amazon Basin had a lifestyle little different from the Stone Age until the time they were contacted by Europeans. However, **archaeological** discoveries in the Upper Xingu territory of Brazil suggest that they lived in large village complexes more like those seen in Europe in the Middle Ages.

Circular cities

The first inhabitants of Mato Grosso in what is now Brazil came from the west about 1,500 years ago. Before the arrival of Europeans, they lived in a complex **urban** (city) system of interconnected population centers that was remarkable for its circular cities protected by high **palisades** of logs. These urban centers may well be the "walled cities" that Francisco de Orellana referred to in 1542.

Population

Today, the remains of about 20 ancient population centers have been located in Upper Xingu. Taken together, these urban centers would fill an area about the size of Belgium and would hold about 50,000 inhabitants.

TYPES

Three types of urban centers were found: cities and ceremonial centers; towns or villages; and living centers without any buildings remaining.

ORIENTATION

The centers are divided by a series of paths. Usually, a main path runs east-west, with secondary paths going north-south.

AVENUES

Large avenues, about 65 feet (19 meters) wide, connected the urban centers. Some may have reached 130 feet (40 meters) wide.

SOUTH AMERICA

BRAZIL

AMAZONIA

Archaeologist Michael Heckenberger used numbers to label the urban centers found in the Upper Xingu. X11, for example, corresponds to Kuhikugu, the most well-preserved site in the region.

AMAZON JUNGLE

River Xingu

X9
X2
X7
X1
X30
X17
X16
X26
X15
X25
X14
X6
X13
X18
X22
X19
X20
X33
X21
X38
X34
X11 (Kuhikugu)
Lake Lamakuka
X35/36

References

- - - Avenues
⊛ Cities that were also ceremonial centers
○ Medium-sized towns
● Centers with no buildings of any kind

Extended area

Mato Grosso

Why Didn't They Create Larger Urban Centers?

Some archaeologists, such as American Jonathan Haas, a curator at the Field Museum in Chicago, believe that city size in the Amazon was limited by natural conditions. "The jungle landscape does not favor centralization of production," he states. Other researchers feel that city size was more likely constrained by boundaries set to maintain political balance between tribal leaders. The fact that the largest urban centers are evenly spaced seems to support this theory.

Kuhikugu, a well-preserved Amazon city

Of all the urban sites in the Amazon, Kuhikugu has provided the most details about the ancient way of life of those who inhabited the Mato Grosso. It reveals that the largest expansion of the indigenous population of Upper Xingu took place between A.D. 1200 and 1400.

The Kuikuro
Some scholars believe the Kuikuro, one of the modern tribes of Mato Grosso, once occupied Kuhikugu. The remains of pottery found at the ancient city seems to support this theory.

Palisade

Double palisade

Fertile soils
The remains of gardens and fields show that the inhabitants were able to make the poor Amazon soil more fertile and productive.

Chief's house

Central Square

Homes

Avenues

Orchard

Access to the lake

Powerful families
Remains of houses show the most influential families of the tribe lived to the northeast and southwest of the city, with the chief always in the center. Their houses were larger than others.

Protection
Remains of tall wooden palisades, or fences, are found at many sites. What did they protect the inhabitants from? They may have helped protect the city from attacks by rival tribes. However, at Kuhikugu, one side of the palisade opens to the lagoon, providing little protection.

Was There a Great Civilization in the Amazon?

Experts increasingly understand that a complex **culture** inhabited the Amazon Basin in ancient times. However, they still do not know whether there was one great civilization widespread throughout the region or if there were several independent kingdoms.

Deforestation in large areas of the Amazon, as well as satellite photography and GPS (Global Positioning System) technology, is helping **archaeologists** investigate the theory that the Amazon Basin was home to an advanced **civilization** in times before European contact. Until recently, most experts considered the Amazon Basin to be an untouched rain forest habitat with jungle plants and mysterious, often dangerous, wildlife. This jungle was a place populated by Stone Age peoples with only simple technology and social organization who struggled to survive on what little food nature offered. **Anthropologists** recognized that these **indigenous** peoples of the Amazon possessed great knowledge of the natural world surrounding them, but they seemed to lack the qualities of a civilization, such as centralized governments, **urban** centers, and an economy based on more than hunting, fishing, and simple farming.

But ideas changed. As anthropologist Michael Heckenberger affirmed, "hidden under the tops of the jungle trees are the signs of a complex **pre-Columbian society.**" Heckenberger has worked among the Kuikuro, the largest tribe in the Upper Xingu of north-central Brazil. This community is one of several that speak various dialects of the same language and form what scientists call the *Caribe subsystem* of the Amazon Basin. In this region, Heckenberger has excavated a network of cities and villages pre-dating European contact that are connected by ancestral highways. These places may once have sustained a population that he thinks may have been 20 times larger than today's. Based on Heckenberger's calculations, the ancestors of the Kuikuro could have constructed walled urban centers that housed up to 50,000 people. He believes that the spacing and organization of these cities indicates a regional planning system. The communities were grouped into towns of about 150 acres (0.6 square kilometers), spread throughout the jungle, and were surrounded by high **palisades,** not unlike communities in Europe during the Middle Ages.

Although housing in these communities was made of perishable wood and thatch rather than stone, for Heckenberger, they are still complex urban centers. His team has mapped several large towns, all of which have a central ceremonial site. Surrounding satellite villages were built in precise positions around the ceremonial site, demonstrating a high level of planning. At least 20 of these population centers have been identified in the Upper Xingu region, and there are likely more to be found in areas that have not yet been mapped. **Radiocarbon** dating suggests that the ancestors of the modern Kuikuro began clearing the

VILLAGE MODEL

A modern-day Kayapo village next to the Iriri River, a tributary of the Xingu in Brazil. The Kayapo were once part of the Xinguana culture, and today their towns are built in the same pattern as those seen in archaeological sites.

The Xinguana Culture

Today, several tribes inhabit the forested region of the Upper Xingu in Brazil. Although the tribes speak different languages, mostly belonging to the Caribe or Tupi-Guarani language families, they share a similar social organization and beliefs and customs. Their villages are built in the shape of large circles with broad avenues leading to the exterior. Together, these tribes make up a larger group that researchers call the Xinguana culture.

Anthropologists studying the oral traditions of the Kuikuro people have determined that they are the descendants of the people who built Kuhikugu and its regional framework, which dates to as far back as A.D. 400, and that other nearby tribes subsequently adopted this model. Some scholars think that the tribes of the Upper Xingu created a league of independent cities rather than a unified culture. This organization may have been designed so that independent kingdoms could cooperate in matters of food and defense.

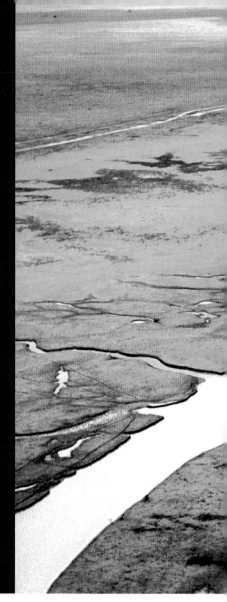

jungle and low-lying areas some 1,500 years ago to build the sites, which are uninhabited today.

Heckenberger also discovered areas dedicated to growing manioc (also called cassava), sweet potatoes, corn, and such semi-domesticated fruits as peach palm and Amazon avocado. This is why he terms these sites "garden cities." They were surrounded by remains of trenches that once held tall palisades constructed of trees. More than 200 enormous avenues and large irrigation canals have been found, as well as the remains of dikes and human-made lakes that could have been used as fish farms. The complex framework of villages and towns, avenues, and other massive structures, which have remained hidden under the dense layers of Amazon vegetation, are even more apparent on satellite images taken from space.

The scientists are not certain if the remains of the "garden cities" found in the Xingu area are at all related to the **geoglyphs,** visible only from the air, that cover large areas of northern Bolivia and western Brazil. However, both demonstrate that large areas of the Amazon were densely populated before the arrival of the first European colonizers after 1492.

AGRICULTURAL TECHNIQUES
Several other lines of evidence have led researchers to conclude that the Amazon region was home to a large, productive society in **pre-Columbian** times. One of the most important forms of evidence is the existence of plots of land covered with *terra preta,* an extremely fertile soil, in certain locations. In a jungle, where soils are typically poor and unsuitable for farming, these plots have been enriched with organic matter and other materials. This enhanced soil would have allowed the farming necessary to support large populations. Researchers believe that as much as 23,000 square miles (60,000 square kilometers) of the Amazon may be covered with this **fertile** soil. The deposits of *terra preta* are particularly abundant along the banks of the Amazon River and on Marajó Island at the mouth of the river. This island was the home of a sophisticated **culture** in pre-Columbian times. However, researchers know almost nothing about the Marajó culture.

Marajó Culture

The large, flat island of Marajó, located in the mouth of the Amazon River, is one of the greatest **archaeological** mysteries of South America. Between around A.D. 400 and 1600, it was the home of an advanced **culture,** but little remains of this culture other than its abundant, sophisticated **ceramics.** They built their homes on artificially raised mounds on this island in the river delta, which is flooded for about half the year. The Marajó culture disappeared some time before the arrival of European explorers. What became of these people remains a mystery.

Kuelap

The fortified enclosure of Kuelap, built by the Chachapoya, lies be-tween the Andes Mountains and the Amazon jungle. The Chachapoya people came from the region of the Andes Mountains but enlarged their territory between the 700's and the 1400's, moving into the rain forest region and encroaching into the Amazon Basin. Scientists know little about the Chachapoya culture, but some re-searchers believe that they controlled busy trade routes between the peoples of the Amazon basin and the Andes, providing indirect evidence of large populations in the Amazon. The Chachapoya were eventually conquered by the Inca and became part of their empire in 1480.

Marajó Ceramics

On the island of Marajó, at the **estuary** of the Amazon, an **indigenous culture** distinguished by its sophisticated **ceramics** flourished between A.D. 400 and 1600. The discovery of the culture in the 1800's was the first indication to scholars that unknown Amazon civilizations existed before European contact.

Funerary Urns

The Marajó culture was known for creating funeral urns to hold the bones of the dead. The urn is often decorated with a stylized representation of the occupant's face. While some urns are clearly **anthropomorphic** (humanlike), others have hybrid features, with elements of both human and animal. Some urns are decorated with the face of an owl. The face of

this bird represents a feminine spirit linked to death. The owl design appears often on urns used to hold female remains. Other common themes on funeral urns include eyebrows and noses that are united in a "T" or "Y" shape. On funeral urns holding male remains, adornments on lips and ears and eyes in the shape of scorpions are common decorations.

EYES IN THE SHAPE OF A SCORPION

Y-SHAPED EYEBROWS

LEDGE
Ledges were a sign of social distinction.

ANTHROPOMORPHIC FEATURES

FEMININE SHAPE
A representation of gender by shape appears most often on female urns.

"COFFEE BEANS"
The owl's semi-closed eyes are represented with semi-spherical protuberances known as "coffee beans."

Burials and Cemeteries

The people of Marajó practiced secondary burials. The dead were placed in a special area where they were allowed to decay. After the flesh rotted away, the bones of the dead were cleaned and placed in a large urn. This custom changed over time. Burial in family plots was common during a time **archaeologists** call the classical period (about A.D. 700 to 1100). This changed during a time archaeologists call the period of decadence (A.D. 1100 to 1300), when bodies were *cremated* (burned) and the burial urns were placed in common graves, as shown in this photograph taken in 1921.

Decorated Dinnerware

The Marajó people left an important ceramic legacy in the form of tableware. Large numbers of plates, drinking vessels, pots, bowls, trays, and other utensils decorated with stylized themes based on plant, animal, or geometric designs have been found at archaeological sites on the island. The artisans used various decorating techniques. These included designs cut into the clay and etched on the exterior faces of plates, bowls, and drinking vessels. Some objects are painted with symmetrical geometric designs. Stylized drawings and geometric shapes are the most prevalent designs on the interior of plates and bowls. The colors used most often in these paintings were white, *ochre* (reddish brown), and black.

RELIEFS

Reliefs and incisions were common designs, as was the addition of append-ages and human or animal heads, in this case, a turtle.

PLATE WITH HEADS

Plate with animal drawings and human heads in red paint.

BOWL WITH AÇAÍ

Some urns contained bowls with carbonized açaí berries.

SHELL-SHAPED

Back of a bowl with grooved decoration inspired by a turtle's shell.

BOTTOM OF PLATE

Plate painted with geometric symbols in yellow tones.

Marajó Bikini

One of the most unusual items found on Marajó Island is ceramic in the form of clothing. Archaeologists at first did not know what these pieces of pottery were, as many were found broken, until some of them were found affixed to anthropomorphic funerary urns representing females. This allowed archaeologists to conclude that the odd-shaped ceramic pieces were actually an item of clothing. The ceramic triangles were a garment worn by women much like a bikini bottom. The corners of the ceramic garment contained holes and grooves where cords holding the item to the body were affixed. Today, one can only wonder how comfortable such clothing could have been.

DESIGNS

Both plain and decorated ceramic "bikini bottoms" have been found. Archaeologists assume that the decorated ones belonged to children and young women.

Did They Enrich the Soil in the Jungle?

Archaeologists have found several plots of extremely **fertile** soil in the Amazon Basin, where nutrient-poor rain forest soils normally are found. This black soil is called **terra preta,** a rich soil mixture created by humans.

Terra preta (Portuguese for black earth) is completely different from the unproductive red or yellow soils that are found in much of the Amazon **Basin.** Plots of this dark material contain large amounts of carbon in the form of *biochar* (burnt plant remains and charcoal that hold water and nutrients). The dark soil also contains large amounts of pottery fragments, animal-bone fragments, fish spines, and turtle shells, as well as human and animal excrement. Researchers believe that this dark soil cannot have formed naturally in the Amazon region. Rain forest soils are typically poor in nutrients and organic materials. Once the rain forest is cleared, the soil is quickly exhausted and becomes unproductive after a few years of farming. Scientists believe *terra preta* must be the result of human activity. Plots of *terra preta* in the Amazon region range from 20 inches (51 centimeters) to more than 6 feet (2 meters) deep, much deeper than other Amazon soils, which usually do not exceed 8 inches (20 centimeters) in depth. Some samples have been **radiocarbon** dated to between 800 B.C. and A.D. 500. The black soil has many interesting qualities: it is very **fertile,** it is highly resistant to decomposition, and it has a great capacity for retaining water and nutrients. Researchers interested in sustainable farming in the Amazon have taken interest in *terra preta.* Experiments have demonstrated that the productivity of *terra preta*, without additional fertilizer, is superior compared to the artificially fertilized soil farmed in the region today.

AGRICULTURAL SOCIETIES

Terra preta was first described at the end of the 1800's by American geologist James Orton, and later by Canadian geologists Charles Hartt and Herbert Smith. However, the promise of this dark material was largely ignored until Dutch soil specialist Wim Sombroek took up residence in Manaus in 1966 to direct an ecological project financed by the World Bank. He later founded an association to promote the development of *terra preta* for use in modern farming.

For archaeologists the biggest questions surrounding *terra preta* remain unanswered. Who created this rich soil mixture? How was it used? Was it invented intentionally to improve soil fertility, a casual discovery, or a by-product of human settlements? Was *terra preta* the secret that allowed people to farm the poor soils of the Amazon Basin?

CHARCOAL

Charcoal is a fundamental ingredient in *terra preta* and gives the soil its dark color.

EXCAVATION

Professor Neves, in cap and dark blue shirt, and his research team show an excavated section of *terra preta* to visitors in Brazil.

ABUNDANCE OF DEPOSITS

Researchers have discovered many deposits of *terra preta* along the banks of the Amazon River in Brazil. The black and white squares on this map show the location of known deposits of *terra preta*.

How the Soil Is Examined

Soil analysis scientists test a soil's **fertility**. This **agricultural** technique has also become a useful instrument for Amazonian **archaeology**. Archaeologists can test the productive capacity of *terra preta* and calculate how many people could have been supported by farming in the Amazon Basin using the material.

Composition analysis

To know the *composition* (makeup), the fertility, and the health of the soil, scientists must analyze its physical, chemical, and biological properties. After a soil sample is taken in the field, its properties are investigated in the laboratory. Scientists analyze several physical qualities of the soil, including the structural stability, ability to hold moisture, and texture. Chemical analysis measures the level of acidity and the proportions of carbon, salt, metals, and other elements in the soil. Biological analyses include determining the amount of *organic* (once living) material present and observing the activity of microbes and earthworms in the material. This information allows soil scientists to determine how well the soil can support the cultivation of food crops.

OXISOL, THE AMAZONIAN SOIL

Scientists call the kind of soil typically seen in the Amazon rain forest **oxisol**. It is a hard, clay-like soil that lacks nutrients and black organic material. The intense tropical rains have washed the nutrients out of the Amazon soil, leaving only insoluble minerals, such as iron oxide and aluminum, which gives the soil its characteristic reddish or yellowish tone. *Terra preta* is an oxisol converted to fertile soil by the addition of materials such as burnt plant remains, charcoal, pottery, and bone.

SAMPLING PROCEDURE

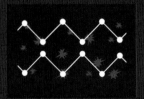

1 **PREPARATION**
A soil scientist collects samples from several locations within an area. In order to obtain a representative sample, they may walk a zigzag path, taking samples every 20 steps along a river bank.

2 **EXCAVATION**
After clearing vegetation from the surface area where the sample will be taken, a shovel is used to make a "V" shaped hole, and a portion of soil approximately 2-3 inches (5 to 7.5 cm) thick is extracted.

3 **SUBSAMPLE**
The sides of the sample are removed and discarded. The remaining soil from the center is placed into a bucket. A soil scientist will take about 6 to 8 subsamples per acre.

4 **MIXING**
All the subsamples are mixed together in the bucket. Then a portion is removed, placed in a bag, and sent to the laboratory for analysis.

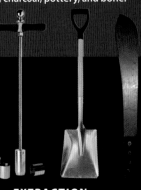

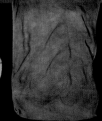

TOOLS

The tools needed for taking soil samples for laboratory analysis are simple. Just a shovel and a bucket will do. For more detailed analysis, a specialized soil borer can be used. Whatever tools are used, there is one absolute requirement: the tools must be clean. Dirty tools can have residues of fertilizer or other soils that could contaminate the samples and invalidate the results of the analysis.

EXTRACTION

A soil borer, straight shovel, and a machete for clearing vegetation are the main tools that scientists use for obtaining soil samples to analyze.

DEPOSIT

Just as with the extraction tools, the bucket must be clean. A tape measure may be used to measure the depth at which samples are taken.

TRANSPORT

Clean plastic bags, cardboard boxes, or burlap sacks are used to transport the samples. These must be labelled so scientists know where they were taken.

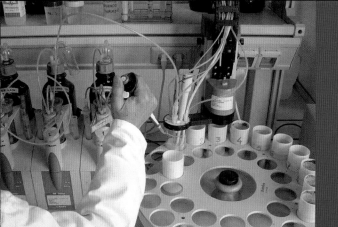

In the Laboratory

After the location of each sample is recorded, the soil samples are dried, crushed in a mortar, and sifted. The samples are then subjected to different chemical analyses. Soil scientists use a variety of laboratory instruments to measure the acidity of the soil and the amount of various elements including calcium, magnesium, phosphorus, potassium, and sodium. Other methods are used to measure the presence of nitrogen and carbon-containing organic materials in the samples. All of this information is used to determine the fertility of the soil and its suitability for farming.

Analyzing age

Archaeologists use carbon-based materials, such as charcoal in the soil, for **radiocarbon dating** (also called Carbon 14 dating). Examining the sequence of layers also helps archaeologists determine how and when *terra preta* was first produced in the region. The transition zone between the oxisol (forest soil) layers and the darker *terra preta* layers indicates when people began growing crops in the Amazon Basin.

TERRA PRETA LAYER

The presence of carbon and other organic material darkens the upper layers and helps distinguish *terra preta* layers from the red oxisols beneath.

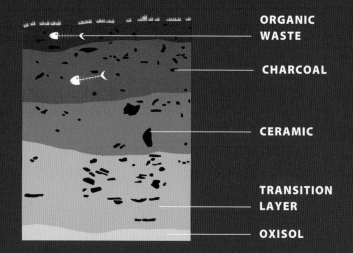

ORGANIC WASTE

CHARCOAL

CERAMIC

TRANSITION LAYER

OXISOL

MEASUREMENTS

An archaeologist measures the depth of a layer of *terra preta* at an excavation site while a colleague takes samples for laboratory analysis.

Who Made the Acre Geoglyphs?

In the Brazilian region of Acre, **deforestation** has revealed enormous symbols cut in the earth, called **geoglyphs.** The meaning of these strange symbols is unknown, but some scholars believe they are the remains of an advanced **culture.**

In the mid-1980's, Brazilian geologist and *paleontologist* (scientist who studies life forms more than 5,500 years old) Alceu Ranzi first observed the massive geoglyphs at Acre while flying over this region near the Bolivia-Peru border. In this zone of the Upper Purús river, a **tributary** of the Amazon, Ranzi first observed a huge double circle seemingly etched into the earth. He later found other, strangely perfect, geometric forms, including long straight lines, rectangles, squares, spirals, and even what seem to be the forms of animals or people. However, it was only possible to see the enormous dimensions of these structures from the air after recent logging had cleared the forest.

Professor Ranzi, along with Martti Pärssinen from the Finland Ibero-American Institute and Denise Schaan from the University of Pará, published a report in which they proposed these geoglyphs were evidence that a complex **pre-Columbian society** once existed in the western Amazon **Basin.** According to the scientists, the precise geometry and size of the geoglyphs—which in some cases reach 980 feet (300 meters) in diameter—proved the existence of a settled and organized society, capable of building these large-scale works.

The geoglyphs were made by people digging trenches 3 feet (1 meter) to 20 feet (6 meters) deep with reinforced walls on both sides. Many of the geoglyphs are connected to each other by roads. Archaeologists have found pottery and stone tools in some of the trenches, while others have no **artifacts** at all. **Radiocarbon** dating of organic remains found in some of the trenches indicates they were likely built sometime before the 1400's. However, the scientists believe people constructed the geoglyphs over the last 2,000 years, and some may have been rebuilt several times.

So far, 290 such earthworks have been found in Acre, along with about 70 others in Bolivia and another 30 in the Brazilian states of Amazonas and Rondônia. In 2015, scientists announced plans to use unmanned aerial vehicles called *drones* to search from above for more geoglyphs hidden in the Amazon jungle.

No one knows exactly why the figures were made or who made them. Ranzi felt that the perfect symmetry of these designs clearly speaks of their symbolic significance. They may have had a **ritual** purpose, or represent the outlines of important ceremonial locations.

FAZENDA COLORADA

Discovered in the plains near the Branco River (Brazil), the Fazenda Colorada geoglyph is one of the most complex. It is composed of several different geometrical shapes, including squares, circles, and diagonal lines. The shapes are best seen from the air.

Current local road

Embankment

Ditch

Mound

Can Amazon Farming Techniques Be Used Today?

Some scientists believe that the farming techniques that allowed large populations to thrive in the Amazon region can be useful for sustainable farming in the same region today.

For most of the 1900's, scholars agreed that the Amazon **Basin** could never have sustained large populations because the poor tropical soils could only allow simple farming. However, research at the Moxos Plains in Bolivia by University of Pennsylvania **archaeologist** Clark L. Erickson and colleagues from the Bolivian Institute of Archaeology has shown that ancient people were able to raise sufficient food by growing such crops as corn and cassava on elevated fields. The scientists also conducted an experimental program that showed such fields can be used for sustainable agriculture in the region in modern times. The climate at Llanos de Moxos makes farming there difficult. The seasons alternate between a long dry season in which moisture is scarce and a short rainy season in which most of the low-lying areas are covered with shallow floodwaters. Yet the prehistoric residents of this area modified the landscape to create a highly productive agricultural system that provided food for thousands of people. They constructed a system of **raised fields,** or flat mounds of earth, built above the flooded plains. Experiments in raised-field farming

began in 1990 at the Biological Station of Beni in Bolivia. Erickson conducted experiments where raised fields were reconstructed and planted with crops. The experiments showed that such raised fields retained water and improved soil **fertility,** producing impressive harvests. They found that the raised fields were easy to maintain and consistently produced quality crops over many planting seasons. Because of this success, the project expanded into **indigenous** communities of the region

Erickson believes a wide area of the Amazon Basin was once farmed using raised-field technology. He thinks that the entire landscape around the state of Beni—thousands of square miles of forest patches surrounded by raised fields and linked by **causeways**—was constructed by a complex, well-populated **society** more than 2,000 years ago.

Scientists now realize that highly productive raised-field farming in the Amazon Basin could have provided the sustainable, high-yield agriculture necessary to feed a large population in a region where Western experts had believed agriculture could not have been used because of nutrient-poor rain forest soils.

FARMING INNOVATION

An experimental raised-field station at Moxos Plains, in northern Bolivia. Scientists now realize that raised-field farming could have provided food for large prehistoric populations that once occupied the Amazon Basin, where few people live today.

Was There a Pre-Columbian Food Crisis?

The rapid disappearance of the Amazon **civilizations** leaves many questions without answers. Some scholars believe that diseases imported by the **conquistadors** were not the only cause of their downfall. Some **archaeologists** believe that the Amazon civilizations might have collapsed because of food shortages caused by overpopulation. Archaeologists believe the native population reached its maximum between the 1100's and 1400's. However, while these people grew crops, they relied on hunting and fishing for much of their protein. With an increasing population, these food sources would have been stretched to the limit. Food shortages may have caused starvation, and competition for resources may have led to warfare and the breakdown of **society.** Some scholars think that early Spanish reports of some natives practicing *cannibalism* (humans eating humans) may actually indicate a serious social crisis taking place immediately prior to the arrival of the explorers. In such a weakened state, the natives would not have been able to resist the sicknesses brought by the Europeans, which finished them off. However, others doubt that food shortages caused the decline of Amazon societies.

PROTEIN
Fish was the main source of protein for the Amazon populations.

Why Did These Civilizations Decline?

After thriving for hundreds of years, the Amazon cultures disappeared quickly. Sicknesses brought by the European conquistadors likely killed large numbers of the region's population.

As we have seen, the evidence accumulated over decades strongly suggests that a vast area of the Amazon **Basin,** from western Brazil along the borders with Colombia, Peru, and Bolivia, to the mouth of the Amazon river at the island of Marajó, was home to several large, complex societies. However, much of this area today is covered with rain forest and sparsely inhabited by people. If such great civilizations once arose in this region, what became of them?

MORTAL EPIDEMICS

Scholars know that Native Americans had no exposure to such European diseases as influenza, measles, and smallpox before the 1400's. These diseases originated in the Old World and never existed in the Americas. As a result, Native Americans had no natural **immunity** against such diseases. The mortality among Native Americans from Old World diseases that were usually not fatal for Europeans was devastating. Scientists believe that such infectious diseases could have been brought inland from populations on coastlines initially visited by Europeans as people fled the plagues, long before any European explorer arrived in lands far

from the coast. Entire villages, towns, and cities were wiped out by disease. In the Amazon, encroaching rain forest would have hidden all traces of these **urban** centers within a few years. The first Europeans to explore the Amazon may have encountered places that had been depopulated by furious **epidemics** long before they arrived.

There are few accounts of the impact of infectious disease on the native peoples of the Amazon. However, accounts from other areas show the devastation. In 1520, smallpox swept through the Aztec empire as Hernán Cortés waited to attack the capital, Tenochtitlan. About 40 percent of the city's population died. Another 20 percent died of starvation when Aztec society collapsed due to so many sick and dying people. Without the devastation of this epidemic, the Spanish would not have been able to so easily conquer the Aztec.

In the Amazon, archaeologists have found signs of a rapid population decrease in the Alto Xingu region of Brazil that occurred sometime in the 1500's. This collapse is most likely related to the spread of disease brought by the Europeans among a population that didn't have the necessary biological defenses to fight these diseases.

Places to See and Visit

OTHER PLACES OF INTEREST

BELEM DE PARÁ
PARÁ, BRAZIL

The capital of the State of Pará, in northeastern Brazil, is home to the Paraense Emílio Goeldi Museum, the oldest institution dedicated to the investigation of the nature and **culture** of the Amazon region. Among other collections, it contains an important collection of **ceramics** from the island of Marajó. In this area there are places where farming still takes place using **terra preta.**

ACRE GEOGLYPHS
ACRE, BRAZIL

Since the 1970's, more than 300 **geoglyphs** have been discovered in this state of the Brazilian Amazon. As with the Nazca lines in Peru, the best way to observe them is from the air. Excursions can be booked through travel agencies in Rio Branco. Since 2011, observation towers have been built in select locations to provide views of the massive geoglyphs.

ISLAND OF MARAJÓ
PARÁ, BRAZIL

Belem is the best departure point to reach the island of Marajó, using local river transport. The island is unique in that, during the rainy season, almost half of its area is flooded. There is an **archaeological** excavation zone near Lake Arari, in the central part of Marajó. On the island, visitors can purchase ceramics and baskets that are hand crafted according to ancient Marajó tradition, visit farms, bathe in the river, or enjoy ocean beaches.

Mato Grosso, Brazil

CUIABÁ

The modern capital of Mato Grosso—located in the center of South America—it is the major point of departure for exploring this zone surrounded by three large **ecosystems:** the Amazon, grasslands, and marshlands. The Cuiabá airport maintains connections with many cities in Brazil, especially with Rio de Janeiro and São Paulo, which in turn connect with the rest of the world.

INDIGENOUS VILLAGES

Not all **indigenous** villages are accessible to tourists. In fact, access to the Xingu National Park itself is tightly regulated. However, there are specialized travel agencies that have all the necessary permits to take groups of tourists to some of the villages inside the park where they can even stay overnight. Visitors can also take in rivers, waterfalls, and the magnificent surroundings of Amazon rain forest.

XINGU NATIONAL PARK
MATO GROSSO, BRAZIL

With more than 7 million acres, this park was created to preserve nature and protect the more than 5,000 indigenous people comprising 14 different ethnic groups living within the region. The park, one of the largest in the world, occupies the northern part of the state of Mato Grasso and contains an enormous variety of wildlife.

UNIVERSITY OF PENNSYLVANIA MUSEUM OF ARCHAEOLOGY AND ANTHROPOLOGY
PHILADELPHIA

In 1931, Vincenzo M. Petrullo began a series of expeditions to South America including Mato Grosso, the headwaters of the Paraguay River, and the Xingu River region in Brazil. His expeditions collected a large variety of objects, ranging from bows, arrows, and spears to ceramics, amulets, and feathered headdresses, all of which can be viewed at the museum in its Americas section.

THE AMERICAN MUSEUM OF NATURAL HISTORY
NEW YORK

The Hall of South American Peoples features the art, tools, technologies, and traditions of the continent's **pre-Columbian** cultures. Here, visitors can see examples of spectacular Amazonian featherwork, including a headdress made from toucan and macaw feathers. The headdress was once by a young man of the Rikbaktsa, an indigenous people of Brazil.

Glossary

Agriculture — The raising of crops and farm animals.

Anthropologist — A scientist who studies human culture.

Anthropomorphic — A representation of the human form in art.

Archaeologist — A scientist who studies the remains of past human cultures.

Artifact — Anything made by human skill or work, such as a tool or weapon.

Basin — All the land drained by a river and the streams that flow into it.

Causeway — A raised road or path, usually built across wet ground or shallow water.

Ceramic — Having to do with pottery, earthenware, or with making them. Ceramic articles are usually made of fired clay.

Civilization — The way of life in a society that features complex economic, governmental, and social systems.

Conquistador — A Spanish conqueror in North or South America, especially during the 1500's.

Chronicle — A record of events in the order in which they happened.

Culture — A term used by social scientists for a way of life. Culture includes a society's arts, beliefs, customs, institutions, inventions, language, technology, and values.

Deforestation — To remove or clear trees from a forest.

Ecosystem — All the living and nonliving things in a given area and the relationships among them.

Embankment — A raised bank of earth or stones used to hold back water or support a roadway.

Engraving — A picture made by cutting a design or image into a flat metal plate. The engraved plate is then used to print the image.

Epidemic — The rapid spreading of a disease so that many people have it at the same time.

Estuary — The broad mouth of a river, into which the ocean tide flows.

Federation — A united league of towns or cities, each of which retains control of its own internal affairs.

Fertile — Able to produce crops (when used about land or soil).

Geoglyph — Large designs marked into the ground by moving or arranging rocks or earth upon the landscape.

Immunity — Resistance to disease.

Indigenous — Originating in the region found; native.

Lagoon — A pond or small lake connected with a larger body of water, such as a river.

Manuscript — A book or other document written by hand.

New World — Another name for the Western Hemisphere, which includes the continents of North America and South America.

Nomadic — A wandering lifestyle.

Oxisol — Weathered soils that are found mainly in the tropical regions. These soils are characterized by high iron and aluminum content and very low fertility.

Palisade — A fence of stakes set firmly in the ground to enclose or defend.

Pre-Columbian — Of or belonging to the period before the arrival of Columbus in America.

Radiocarbon — A method of determining the age of an archaeological specimen, such as a bone or piece of wood, by measuring the amount of carbon 14 left in the object.

Raised field — An artificial platform of soil built to farm crops on. They are generally found in areas of seasonal flooding. The mounds of soil with canals for drainage increase the depth of fertile topsoil available to plants.

Ritual — A solemn or important act or ceremony, often religious in nature.

Society — People living together as a group.

Survey — To measure land for size, shape, position, or boundaries so as to draw a map.

Terra preta — Portuguese for "black earth." A rich, black material consisting of charcoal, burnt plant remains, organic material, bones, shells, and pottery fragments, used to increase the fertility of tropical soils in the Amazon region.

Tributary — A stream or river that flows into a larger river or body of water.

Urban — Having the essential characteristics of a city or town.

For Further Information

Books

Abrams, Dennis. *El Dorado*. New York: Chelsea House, 2012. Print.

Fullman, Joe. *Ancient Civilizations*. New York: DK Pub., 2013. Print.

Ganeri, Anita, and David West. *Lost in the Bermuda Triangle and Other Mysteries*. New York: Rosen Central, 2012. Print.

Walker, Kathryn, and Brian Innes. *Mysteries of the Ancients*. New York: Crabtree, 2010. Print.

Weil, Ann. *The World's Most Amazing Lost Cities*. Chicago: Raintree, 2012. Print.

Websites

Amos, Jonathan. "Drone to Scan for Ancient Amazonia." *BBC News*. BBC, 13 Feb. 2015. Web. 24 Feb. 2015.

Cooper, Jago. "The Quest for the Real El Dorado." *BBC News Magazine*. BBC, 13 Jan. 2013. Web. 24 Feb. 2015.

"Explorer: The Search for El Dorado." *National Geographic Explorer*. National Geographic, 2015. Web. 24 Feb. 2015.

Romero, Simon. "Once Hidden by Forest, Carvings in Land Attest to Amazon's Lost World." *The New York Times*. The New York Times, 14 Jan. 2012. Web. 24 Feb. 2015.

Index

Acknowledgments

Pictures:

© ACI

© Album

© Age Fotostock

© Alamy Images

© Cordon Press

© Getty Images

© Science Source

© Shutterstock

The images of the Acre geoglyphs on p. 37 are courtesy of Marti Pärssinen, Iberoamerican Institute of Finland.

The images of two pottery urns from Marajó Island on p. 30 (Photographer: Jeff Wells), are courtesy of Frederick and Jan Meyer, and the digital files of these images are courtesy of the Denver Art Museum.

The image of the raised field on p. 39 is courtesy of Dr. Clark L. Erickson.